BABY-SITTERS LITTLE SISTER®

Karen's Worst Day

BABY-SITTERS LITTLE SISTER®

Karen's Worst Day

ANN M. MARTIN
ILLUSTRATIONS BY CHRISTINE ALMEDA

SCHOLASTIC INC.

This book is for
Read Marie Marcus,
Josh's little sister

This book was originally published in paperback in 1989.

ISBN 978-93-5471-064-3

First printing 2021
This reprint edition, March 2025

Book design by Maeve Norton

Printed in India at Saurabh Printers Pvt. Ltd.

CHAPTER 1

Hi! I am Karen Brewer. I am six. I have a cast on my arm. I broke my wrist two weeks ago. I was roller-skating. I had to go to the hospital and everything.

Daddy and my big stepsister Kristy took me to the hospital. That was because I was at Daddy's house for the weekend. See, my little brother Andrew and I live sometimes with Daddy, and most of the time with Mommy.

Daddy and Mommy used to be married. Then they got divorced. Then they each got married again. Daddy married Elizabeth, and Mommy married Seth. That's how come Andrew and I live in two different houses.

The little house is Mommy's. Andrew and

I live there most of the time. (Andrew is four, by the way. And he is very shy.) We live there with Mommy and Seth and Rocky and Midgie. Rocky is Seth's cat. Midgie is his dog. Seth likes animals and kids, which is lucky for Andrew and me.

The big house is Daddy's. Andrew and I live there every other weekend, and for two weeks in the summertime. Boy, is the big house big. And boy, is it full of people. Here's who lives at the big house besides Andrew and me: Daddy, Elizabeth, Elizabeth's kids, and Shannon and Boo-Boo. Shannon is a puppy. Boo-Boo is Daddy's fat, old cat. He scratches and bites and goes wild. He is not very pleasant.

Elizabeth has four kids. They are my stepbrothers and stepsister. Two of them are terribly old. They are Charlie and Sam and they go to high school. One of my stepbrothers is almost my age. David Michael. He's seven. David Michael and I fight a lot. Then there is Kristy. Kristy is one of my favorite, favorite people.

She's thirteen. Sometimes she baby-sits for Andrew and David Michael and me.

Andrew and I have two houses and two families and two of lots of other things. We each have two pairs of blue jeans and two pairs of sneakers and two bicycles—one for the big house, one for the little house. We have books at Mommy's and books at Daddy's. We have toys at Mommy's and toys at Daddy's. This is so we don't have to take a lot of stuff back and forth when we go from one house to the other.

I even have two stuffed cats—Moosie and Goosie. Moosie stays at the big house, Goosie stays at the little house. For a long time I had a problem, though. My special blanket is Tickly,

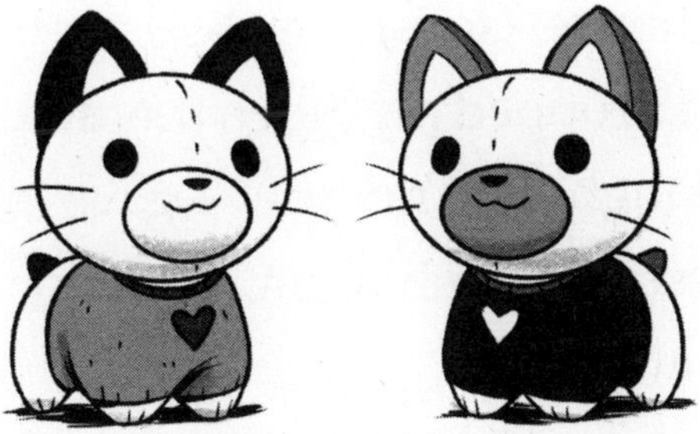

and there was only one Tickly. Sometimes I would forget to bring Tickly with me. Once, I was climbing into bed at Daddy's and I remembered Tickly was at Mommy's. I cried. Having two houses and two families is fun sometimes, but not all the time. Anyway, finally I tore Tickly in half. Now I keep half at each house.

One thing I don't have two of is roller skates. I only have one pair. But that won't matter for a long time. The doctor said no more roller-skating until the cast comes off my wrist. And it won't come off for weeks.

Darn.

Why did I have to fall and break my wrist anyway? I think that was the beginning of my bad luck. I have had some bad luck lately. At Mommy's house, Goosie was lost for two whole days. And I dropped my lunch tray at school and everyone laughed. And after I gave Andrew a very interesting new haircut, Mommy and Seth were mad at me.

But those were just little bits of bad luck. I did

not have a lot of bad luck until Saturday, when Andrew and I were back at the big house. That was one long bad-luck day. It was my worst day ever. In fact, it began the night before, when I was trying to fall asleep. I just could not go to sleep. Even with Moosie and Tickly next to me.

I tried and tried and tried. . . .

CHAPTER 2

Daddy!" I called. "Daddy!"

Daddy was at my door in a flash.

"Karen, what's wrong?" he exclaimed. "Are you sick? Did you fall out of bed?"

"No," I answered. "I can't fall asleep. I can't sleep at all. I've been lying here for hours and hours."

"Honey, Kristy put you to bed twenty minutes ago," Daddy told me.

"Really?" I said. "Well, it seems like hours. Besides, I can see the witch out my window. And she's up to something."

I think I forgot to tell you about my witch. She lives next door. All the grown-ups say she is just an old lady who wears funny black clothes.

They call her Mrs. Porter. But I know better. I know she is not *just* an old lady. And I know she has a witch name. Her witch name is Morbidda Destiny. Morbidda Destiny can cast spells. She has an herb garden in her backyard. That's where she grows things with strange names to use in her spells. Things like fennel and basil.

Morbidda Destiny has a black cat, too. His name is Midnight. Midnight's eyes are round and yellow. They stare at you. Our cat Boo-Boo does not like Midnight, but he especially does not like Morbidda Destiny. Every time he sees her, he does something weird, like race up a tree and stay there, as if his feet were glued to the trunk.

Lots of times, I've seen a broom next to Morbidda Destiny's front door. And she cackles like this, "Heh, heh, heh," and talks to Midnight. And once I think I saw her fly out one of her windows on her broom. But I am not sure about that.

"Karen," said Daddy, "how many times do I

have to tell you? Mrs. Porter is not a witch. She is just—"

"I know," I interrupted him. "She is just an old lady who wears funny black clothes . . . and has a broom and a black cat."

Daddy sighed. Then he pulled down my window shades.

"No more spying on Mrs. Porter," he said. "If you stop thinking about her, you will fall asleep much faster."

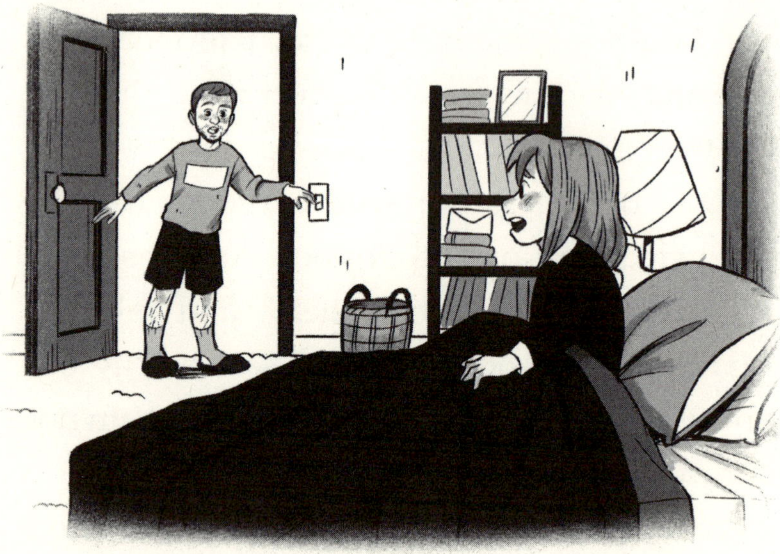

"Okay."

"Think pleasant thoughts and you will have pleasant dreams." Daddy kissed my nose and I gave him a butterfly kiss with my eyelashes.

When he left my room, I thought very pleasant thoughts. And I did go to sleep. But I kept waking up. Each time I did, I looked at my clock. Eleven-thirty, 1:28, 3:44, 5:16, 6:59. . . .

After 6:59, I was running out of pleasant thoughts. I had already thought of ice cream and cartoons and pets and new shoes and birthdays. What was left? . . . Oh! Roller-skating.

I closed my eyes. I pictured myself in my fancy red skates, skating up and down our sidewalk.

My mind began to float away, and soon I was skating in a dream.

In the dream, I reached the end of our sidewalk and saw that I had come to a hill.

If I could just skate up that hill, I thought, then I could go zooming down the other side. The hill was very steep, but a rabbit came along and said, "I will help you reach the top." And he did. He pushed me right up.

"Thank you," I said, but the rabbit was already gone.

I peeked over the hill to see what the road looked like on the other side. There was no road—just a cliff!

Oh, well, I thought. Then I will turn around and coast down the way I came up. But before I could do that, I lost my balance.

I was falling, falling, falling. . . .

CHAPTER 3

Aughhh!" I screamed.

I had landed on the rocky ground. No, I wasn't outdoors. I was in my own bedroom. My skates were gone, the hill was gone, and I was sitting on my rug.

I had fallen out of bed. My pillow was with me. So was Tickly. I checked my cast. It looked okay. Luckily, my arm did not hurt.

"Karen!" Kristy burst into my room. She was wearing her nightgown but she looked wide awake. That was when I realized that the long night was finally over. Sunshine was peeking around my window shades. My clock said 8:15.

Eight-fifteen! The last time I had looked at my clock it had said 6:59.

"What happened?" Kristy cried. She ran to me and sat down on the floor. I crawled into her lap. "How did you fall out of bed?" she asked. "Is your arm okay?"

It was scary falling out of bed with my cast on, but my dream had been even scarier. "My arm is fine," I told Kristy. "But I didn't just fall, I fell off a cliff."

"You were dreaming."

"I know. It seemed real, though."

"Tell me about your dream."

So I told Kristy about the roller skates and the disappearing rabbit and the hill and the cliff. "There *was* no other side of the hill," I explained. "So I tried to turn around, but instead, I lost my balance and fell."

"Right out of bed," Kristy added. "Poor Karen."

"Did I wake you up?" I asked. "I'm sorry if I did."

Kristy shook her head. "I was still in bed, but I was reading. Even if you *had* woken me

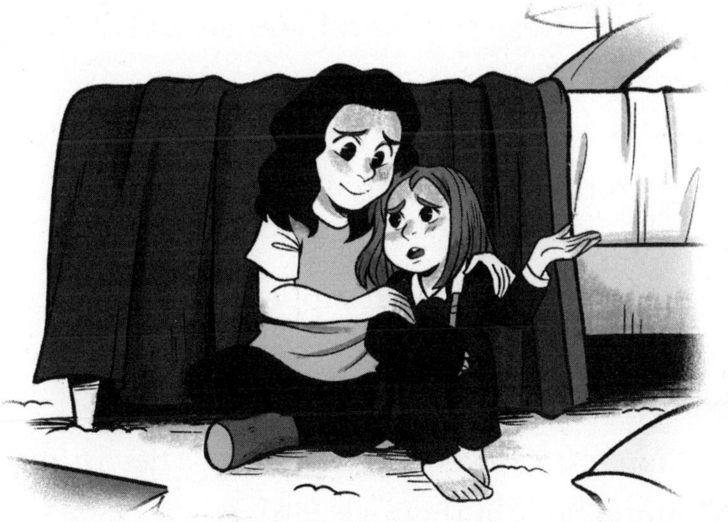

up, I wouldn't have minded. Everyone has bad dreams sometimes."

See why Kristy is one of my favorite people? Andrew and I are very lucky that she is our stepsister.

I got to my feet. I pulled up one of my window shades and sunshine streamed into the room.

"It's a gorgeous day," said Kristy. "It started off badly for you, but I'm sure things will get better now."

"Me, too," I replied.

"Why don't you get dressed? I'll help you."

(I can dress myself, of course, but it is not easy with the cast.)

"Okay," I said. "I think I will wear my red shirt and my new jeans. The ones with the zippers up the sides."

"The ones with the zippers up the sides?" repeated Kristy. "I don't think I've seen those before."

"No, you haven't," I agreed. "They're new. Mommy bought them yesterday."

"Where are they?" asked Kristy.

"In my knapsack," I replied.

Kristy looked through the things in my knapsack. "I don't see them," she said. She handed me the knapsack and I looked through it, too. No jeans.

"I must have left them at Mommy's!" I wailed. "Darn!"

"Oh, well," said Kristy. "Listen, I have an idea. Put on your pink sweat shirt and your regular jeans and your white sneakers. Then I'll surprise you."

I grinned. A surprise? I love surprises! I let Kristy help me into my clothes.

"Now wait right here," said Kristy.

I waited. While I waited, I made my bed. (I had to do it one-handed.) Then I kissed Moosie good-morning.

A few minutes later, Kristy came back. She was wearing jeans and white sneakers and a pink sweat shirt, too. "See? We're twins!" she cried.

"Neat!" I said.

But I still wished for my zipper jeans . . . and that I had not fallen out of bed.

CHAPTER 4

Kristy and I went downstairs and into the kitchen.

Daddy, Elizabeth, Andrew, and David Michael were already there. They were eating breakfast.

"Well, well," said Daddy. "Look at our twins!"

I grinned. I felt very grown-up being Kristy's twin.

"They're not really twins," scoffed David Michael. "Real twins are exactly the same age."

"No way!" I said. "Real twins are *not* exactly the same age. They can't be. One has to be born first. So one is always a few minutes older. In my class at school there are twins, Terri and Tammy. And Terri is a whole half an *hour* older than Tammy. So there."

"Sheesh," said David Michael. "That is not what I meant. What I meant—"

"A-*hem,*" interrupted Daddy. "That's enough. Kristy, Karen, are you hungry?"

"I am," said Kristy.

"I'm *starving,*" I announced. "And I know what I want to eat—Crunch-O cereal."

"Too bad," said Andrew. "I just finished the box—*and* I got the prize!"

My mouth dropped open. I looked helplessly at Daddy and Elizabeth. "You finished the box *and* you got the prize?" I said to Andrew.

He nodded.

"What was the prize?"

"Tattoos."

"Tattoos! That's the best prize of all!"

"We can share," said Andrew.

"Thanks," I replied glumly. I sat down at the table. I put my chin in my hands. I had been all set for Crunch-O.

"Karen," said Elizabeth.

"Yeah?"

Elizabeth stood up. She went to the cupboard. "Look what I have," she said.

I looked. "Oh! A new box of Crunch-O! Thank you, Elizabeth! Thank you!" I jumped up. "Please can I look for the prize?" I asked her. "*Please?* Since Andrew got the other one."

"Well . . . I suppose so."

"Oh, goody! Thank you!"

Elizabeth got out a mixing bowl. She helped me pour the Crunch-O into it. We poured and poured and poured—and at last the prize package slid out. I reached for it. I was about to open it when I realized something. Elizabeth had been awfully nice. I should help her put the cereal back in the box. So I held the box while Elizabeth carefully poured the cereal in it.

Then I poured a bowl of Crunch-O for myself and added some milk.

I sat down at the table with my cereal and the prize package.

I took one bite of cereal—and couldn't wait any longer. I opened the package.

It was empty!

"It's empty!" I cried.

"Oh, no. Someone at the cereal company must have made a mistake," said Daddy.

I stared at the empty package in dismay. "Those mean, bad Crunch-O people," I said.

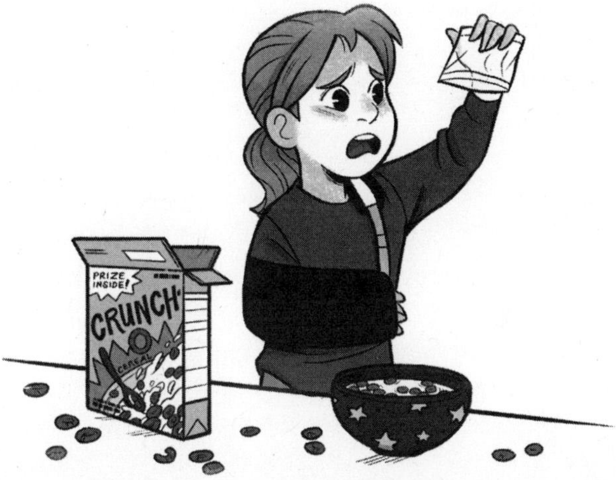

"Hey, Karen, you can still share my prize," Andrew spoke up. "I'll give you half the tattoos, okay?"

"Okay. Thank you."

Andrew was going to share his prize with me, but I did not have a prize of my own. And Kristy and I were twins, but I did not have my zipper jeans. So far, the day was not very good. In fact, it was half bad. What would it be like if it were all bad? I wondered.

CHAPTER 5

When breakfast was over, I wandered into the den. I sat in a chair and pulled my knees up. I rested my chin on them. So far, Saturday did not seem like a very good day. I looked at my watch. Nine twenty-five. It was still early! There was plenty of time for the bad day to turn into a good one.

Maybe a funny TV show is on *right now,* I thought. And that was when I remembered *Mr. Ed. Mr. Ed* is the old black-and-white show about the talking horse. A man sings a funny song like this: "A horse is a horse, of course, of course." And then Mr. Ed says, "I am Mr. Ed."

Mr. Ed makes me giggle.

And *Mr. Ed* reruns come on our TV every

Saturday and Sunday morning at nine-thirty.

I was just about to get up and turn on *Mr. Ed* when Andrew ran into the den. He ran right over to the TV set. He turned it on. He switched it to Channel 5.

KA-POW! BLAM-BLAM-BLAM!

Andrew was watching cartoons.

I hate cartoons. At least, I hate the cartoons that Andrew likes. The only one I like is *Muppet Babies.* Or cartoons with animals and fairies in them.

"Andrew," I said, "*Mr. Ed* is on now."

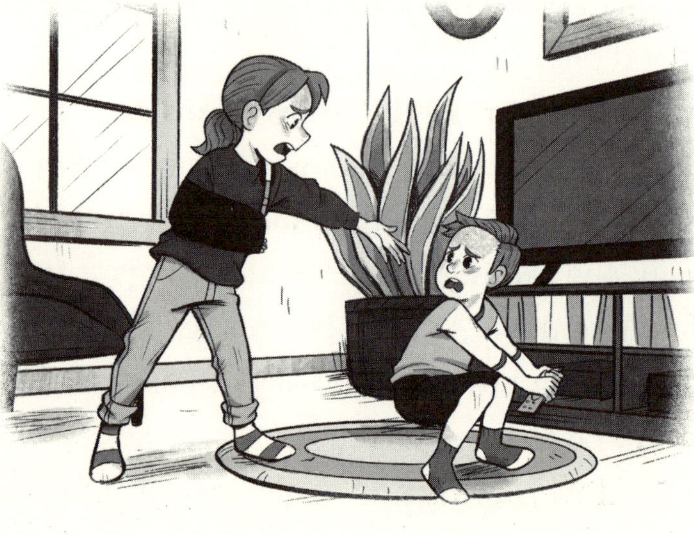

Andrew had plopped himself on the floor right in front of the set. "So?" he replied.

"So I was going to watch it."

"Well, I'm watching cartoons."

"But I want to watch *Mr. Ed*."

"But I want to watch cartoons."

"You can't."

"I already am."

I jumped out of my chair. I ran over to the TV so I could switch the channel.

"Noooo!" howled Andrew, leaping to his feet. "Leave it alone. I got here first."

"Did not."

"Did too."

"Did not. Didn't you see me sitting right there?" I pointed to the chair.

"Yes. But the television was off."

"So what? I—"

"Hey, hey, *hey*!" exclaimed Daddy. He strode into the den. He was taking very big steps, which meant he was cross. Or at least not happy. "What is going on in here?"

"I wanted to watch *Mr. Ed*," I told Daddy, "but Andrew turned on these dumb cartoons."

"Andrew, how long is your cartoon show?" asked Daddy.

Andrew shrugged. Daddy opened the *TV Guide*. "It's an hour long," he announced. "*Mr. Ed* is only half an hour long. Karen, you may watch *Mr. Ed*. After that, Andrew, you may watch the rest of your show. That way you'll each get to see a half an hour of the show you like. Now, no more arguments."

Daddy left the room.

Wow! I thought. Great! Finally some good luck! I could watch *Mr. Ed* after all. Even though I was glad about that, I stuck my tongue out at Andrew. I couldn't help it. He had made me mad.

I switched the channel. I switched it just in time to hear an announcer say, "In order that we may bring you the following special program, *Mr. Ed* will not be seen this morning. It will return tomorrow at the regularly scheduled time."

"Oh, no!" I cried. "Boo. *Mr. Ed* isn't on."

Even the TV people were giving me bad luck.

I looked at Andrew. Then I switched the TV back to his show. "You can watch your cartoons, I guess," I told him.

"Thanks," replied Andrew. "You can still have half the tattoos."

"Thanks."

I left the den. I looked at my watch. Nine thirty-one. There was still time for the bad day to turn into a good day.

CHAPTER 6

I wandered onto our back porch. I sat there with my chin in my hands, and looked out at our yard. The morning was cool and fresh. With the sun shining down, I would not even need to put on a jacket. My sweatshirt would be warm enough.

I watched a squirrel chase another squirrel around and around, up a tree trunk, until they both disappeared in the branches. Then I watched two birds swoop low over the lawn. The animals seemed to be having fun.

Oh! Maybe that was what I needed—one of our pets. An animal can be a very good friend on a bad day.

I jumped up. I was all set to give the day another try. It was still only 9:45. I began to smile as I ran back inside to get Shannon or Boo-Boo. Maybe *now* would be the beginning of the good part of the day.

I found both Shannon and Boo-Boo in the living room. They were asleep on a couch. It's funny—Boo-Boo is a cross old cat, but he is always nice to Shannon. Even when Shannon is frisking around, teasing Boo-Boo, Boo-Boo never hisses or swipes at her. And when they are both tired, they take naps together.

I think it is very nice of Boo-Boo to be so kind to Shannon.

Just because Boo-Boo is nice to Shannon, though, does not mean he is nice to people. In fact, Boo-Boo is weird. He's always running and hiding, or scratching and biting.

If I wanted to play with a nice pet, it would be Shannon. But there were a couple of problems with that. For one thing, Shannon is really David

Michael's dog. She does not know Andrew and me very well because she does not see us too often. For another thing, Shannon was asleep.

I lifted Shannon's ear. "Oh, Shannon," I whispered into it.

Shannon opened her eyes.

"Good," I said. "You're awake. Come on outside and play with me."

Shannon was a *very* sleepy puppy, but I scooped her up and took her outside with me. Right away, she woke up.

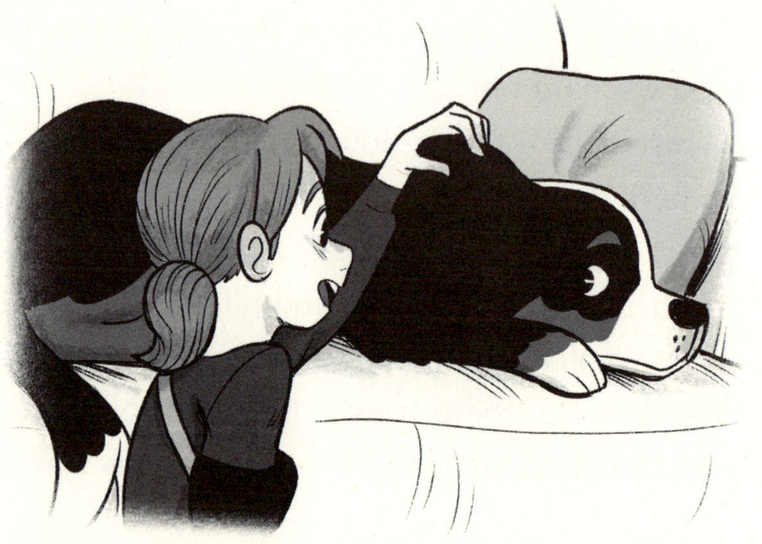

"Come on, Shannon! Chase me!" I cried.

Shannon chased after me. Then I threw a stick and she fetched it. I threw a ball and she fetched that, too.

Then I threw the stick again, but Shannon could not find it. She looked and looked.

"That's okay, Shannon," I called. "You don't have to find that stick. I'll throw another one for you." But Shannon would not stop snuffling around, looking for the stick.

Well, this was no fun.

Then David Michael came outside.

"Shannon!" he called.

Shannon ran to him. She forgot all about the stick *and* me.

I felt tears prick at my eyes, but I blinked them back. I'll just go and get Boo-Boo, I thought. So I did. It was not easy. Boo-Boo hissed at me because he did not want to be picked up. But I hauled him outside anyway.

"Okay, let's play," I said to Boo-Boo.

Boo-Boo did not look at me. He was staring

at . . . Morbidda Destiny! She was in her herb garden next door.

"Hsss!" went Boo-Boo, and he ran up a tree.

"Ha, ha, ha, ha, ha!" laughed David Michael.

But I did not laugh. Nothing seemed funny to me.

CHAPTER 7

I ran to the tree that Boo-Boo had climbed.

"Boo-Boo!" I called. "Boo-Boo! Come on down."

Boo-Boo was not listening. He had reached a high branch in the tree and was balancing on it.

I looked over at David Michael. He was throwing the ball for Shannon. They were having lots of fun. David Michael had forgotten about Boo-Boo and me. So had Shannon.

Well, I could have fun, too. If I could just get Boo-Boo down, we could play and have a good time . . . couldn't we?

"Boo-Boo!" I called again. "Come down from there!" Then I added very softly, "Morbidda

Destiny isn't going to hurt you." (I didn't want the witch to hear me.)

Boo-Boo did not even look at me.

Ah-*ha*! I thought. Cat food! That always works. On TV when a cat is up a tree, someone puts a dish of food on the ground, and the cat comes down to eat. Simple!

I ran inside and poured Boo-Boo's favorite crunchy food into a saucer. Boo-Boo had just eaten breakfast, but so what. He had not eaten his crunchy food. He would want a treat.

I ran back outside and over to Boo-Boo's tree.

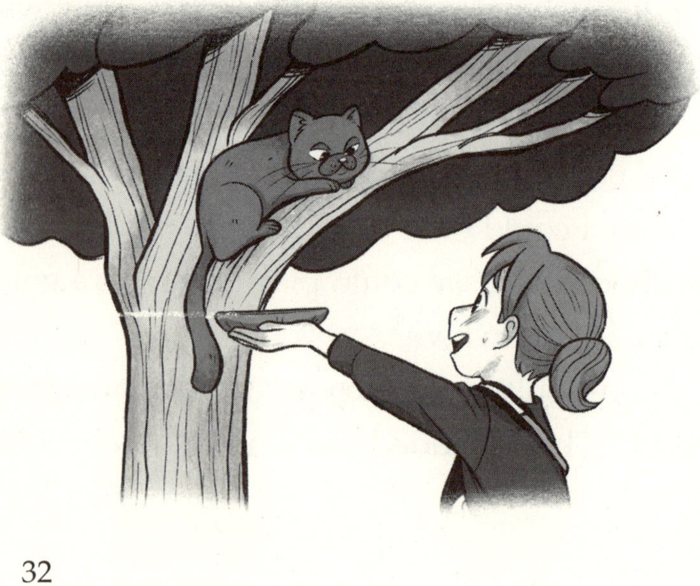

"Hey, Boo-Boo!" I called. "Look what I have for you!" I held up the dish of cat crunchies so Boo-Boo could see it.

He blinked his eyes. He stayed put.

I set the dish on the ground and waited. Nothing happened. Boo-Boo looked like he might be getting ready to doze off. There was only one thing to do. I began to climb the tree. It was not easy, one-handed. But there were lots of limbs to step on.

Boo-Boo woke up. He watched me climb toward him. He moved away from me.

Then, "Karen Brewer! You come down from that tree this instant!"

It was Daddy. He was shouting to me from the kitchen window.

I backed down. I hadn't gotten very far anyway.

"Boo-Boo!" I called one more time. And then I gave up. I sat down next to the cat crunchies.

Right away, Boo-Boo began edging down the tree. All *right!* I thought. But I did not say anything. I knew that if I did, Boo-Boo would stay in the tree, just to make me mad. Instead, I watched Morbidda Destiny working in her garden. She looked very busy.

Suddenly, two things happened at once. Boo-Boo jumped to the ground. And in her garden, the witch exclaimed crossly, "Oh, fiddlesticks!" She began waving a rake around. Boo-Boo took one look at her and raced for the house.

Fiddlesticks. Was that a magic witch word? A spell for cats? Had Morbidda Destiny put a spell on Boo-Boo?

I didn't stay around to find out. I ran after Boo-Boo. If David Michael had any sense, he would come inside, too. And he would bring Shannon with him.

The witch was on the loose!

CHAPTER 8

David Michael did run inside. And he did bring Shannon with him. But I think he waited too long. I think Morbidda Destiny put a spell on him.

Why do I think this? Because David Michael got really mean.

The first thing he said after he had closed the door behind him was, "Mo-om! I'm going over to Linny's."

"All right!" Elizabeth called back.

Linny Papadakis is David Michael's good friend. He and his family live across the street from us and one house down. Linny has two younger sisters. Sari is really little, but Hannie is my age, and she is my best friend. Well, she is my best friend when I am at the big house. When I am at the little house, I have a different best friend. (Her name is Nancy.)

Suddenly I felt like playing with Hannie. Maybe that would make my day better.

"I'm going with David Michael!" I called.

"No, you're not," he replied just as Elizabeth said, "Okay!"

"Yes, I am."

"No, you're not." (See how mean he was being?)

"Yes, I *am*. I want to see Hannie. I can go over there if I want."

"Okay, but don't go with me."

"David Michael!"

Ding-dong.

David Michael and I both ran for the front door. We reached it at the same time. We had a fight over who would get to open it.

David Michael won. (I bet he wouldn't have won if he had a cast on *his* arm.)

Standing at the door were Hannie and Linny.

"Hi!" I said. "Guess what. We were just coming over to see *you*."

"You *were?*" said Hannie. "Good. That means you're free."

"Free?" I repeated.

"To go bike riding."

"Yeah," said Linny. "We're riding to Harry's Brook. We're going to look for water spiders, and catch minnows and crayfish. We even brought sandwiches for lunch."

"And cookies!" added Hannie. "A real picnic."

"Neat!" exclaimed David Michael. "Let me ask Mom if I can go."

David Michael ran off, but I just stood there. I glared at Hannie. Finally I said, "Well, thanks a lot."

"What's wrong?" asked Hannie.

"What's wrong?" I repeated. "What's *wrong*?! You know I can't go bike riding. That's what's wrong. I'm not allowed to ride my bike until my cast comes off. And I can't go wading in brooks,

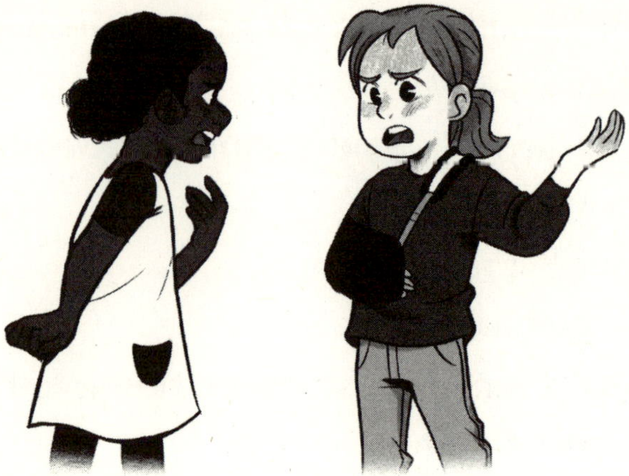

either. I might get the cast wet. How could you be so mean, Hannie? You are a toad!" Hannie was mean, too. Maybe *she* was under the witch's spell.

"I am not!" yelled Hannie.

"Are so!"

"Am not so!"

"Are so too!"

"Am not so too!"

"Okay! I can go!" David Michael had come back. He was holding a bag of apples. "Mom gave us these for the picnic," he said. "Let's get our bikes."

David Michael and Linny left, but Hannie stayed behind. "You called me a toad," she said. "I'm *glad* you can't come with us. We wouldn't want you."

"Well, I wouldn't want to go on a picnic with a toad. So there!" I replied.

Hannie turned her back on me. I closed the front door. Why wasn't my bad day getting better? Was it all Morbidda Destiny's fault? Or was I just having an awful, rotten day?

CHAPTER 9

After I closed the door, I stood in our hallway for a few moments. The house was quiet. Elizabeth was in the den, sewing. Sam and Charlie were over at a friend's house. David Michael had gone on his stupid picnic. And Daddy had taken Andrew downtown for a haircut.

Where was Kristy? Where was my twin?

"Kristy?" I called.

"I'm in the kitchen!" she replied.

I found Kristy putting a batch of brownies in the oven. "Hi, twin," she said.

"Hi," I answered. "What are those for?"

"The Baby-sitters Club. I'm going to bring them to our next meeting." Kristy does so much baby-sitting that she and her friends have a baby-sitting club.

"Oh."

Kristy closed the oven door. "Want to play?" she asked.

I had a feeling Kristy was just being nice to me, but I did want to play with her, so I said, "We could play checkers." I am good at checkers.

"Okay," replied my sister.

We found the checkers and set up the game in Kristy's room. She has a gigantic bed. It's big enough so that we could put the game in the middle and lie on our stomachs if we wanted to. That is a very comfortable way to play checkers.

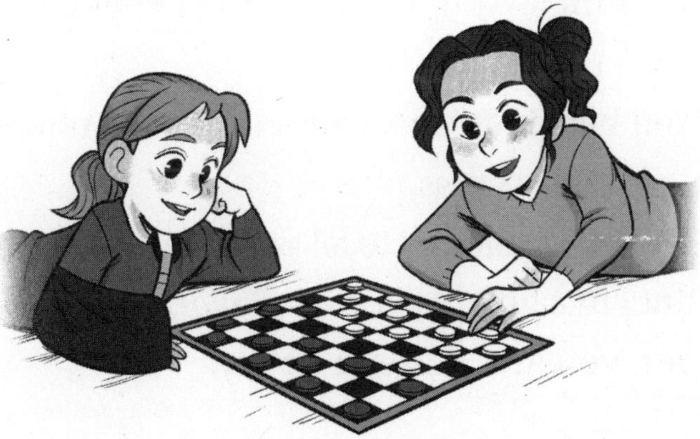

"You go first," Kristy said.

I smiled. "Thanks!" That was nice of her. Kristy was not a toad.

The game began. I did a lot of jumping. Once, I got a triple jump. Jump, jump, jump. Three of Kristy's pieces became mine. And *my* pieces were slowly crowned. They were made kings.

I gave Kristy a stern look. "Now don't *let* me win," I said to her. "I hate when big people do that."

Kristy blushed. "Sorry, Karen. Okay. I'll play my best from now on. I promise."

The next thing I knew, Kristy got a triple jump. Jump, jump, jump. Then two of her pieces became kings. And the *next* thing I knew, Kristy had won the game.

"You beat me!" I exclaimed. I could not help looking a little cross.

"Well, you said not to let you win. So I didn't."

"But I'm a good checkers player," I protested.

"Yes, you are," agreed Kristy.

"Then how come I didn't win?"

Kristy sighed. She began to look more like a grown-up and less like my big sister. "Do you want to play again?" she asked. "Maybe you'll win this time."

"Okay," I said.

We set up the board for a second game. Then we started to play. Kristy played very badly.

But I got jumps and double jumps and triple jumps.

"King me! King me!" I said each time one of my pieces reached Kristy's side of the board.

After awhile all of my pieces were kings and none of Kristy's were. Plus, I had jumped half of her pieces.

"You're not letting me win again, are you?" I asked.

"Well, I—I, um . . ."

"You are! You are letting me win!" I cried.

"But you were upset when I beat you."

"But I didn't want you to let me win!"

"Karen, I'm sorry. I'm really sorry," Kristy began.

I didn't hear what she said next, though. I had run out of her room.

CHAPTER 10

I needed to hug something, so I went looking for Shannon. Now that David Michael was gone, maybe she would play with me. But Shannon was asleep. She was probably all tired out from playing with mean David Michael. And Shannon is only good for hugging and playing when she is awake. So I left Shannon where I found her—curled up in the living room with Boo-Boo.

I went upstairs to my room. I would just have to hug Moosie and Tickly instead. I could play with them, too. They are not as much fun as Shannon and Boo-Boo are, but then, it was my bad day, so what did I expect?

I closed the door to my bedroom.

Then I ran across my room and leaped onto my bed. "Hello, Moosie-Moosie," I said. I gave Moosie a *very* tight squeeze.

Then I spread Tickly on the bed. I wrapped Moosie up in Tickly.

"Now you look just like a baby," I told Moosie.

I rocked Moosie in my arms for awhile.

"Did you ever have a bad day? An awful day?" I asked Moosie.

Moosie looked at me with his round button eyes.

"Probably not," I answered myself. "A real cat might have a bad day, but not a stuffed one.

"You know what's happened so far today, Moosie? Everything. I had a bad dream, I fell out of bed, I forgot my jeans, the Crunch-O prize package was empty, *Mr. Ed* wasn't on, Shannon wouldn't play with me, Boo-Boo ran up a tree, I had a fight with Hannie, and Kristy treated me like a baby. I think the witch is practicing her spells."

I put Moosie back on the bed and unwrapped Tickly. "I think you need a new outfit, Moosie," I said.

I lifted up Moosie's T-shirt. Underneath I found a big rip. Moosie's stuffing was coming out!

I ran to my door and flung it open. "Elizabeth! Elizabeth!" I called.

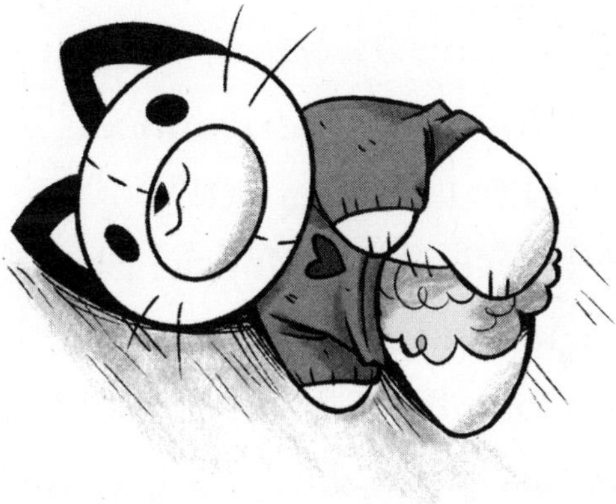

CHAPTER 11

Elizabeth came running. "Karen, what's the matter?" she cried.

I took Elizabeth by the hand and pulled her to my bed.

"Look at Moosie!" I exclaimed. "He's sick! He's dying! He's falling apart!"

Elizabeth picked up Moosie. She poked his stuffing back inside his tummy. She looked at the rip for a long time. Then she said, "I am the animal doctor, Karen. Do you give me permission to operate on Moosie?"

"I guess so," I replied.

"He'll have a scar," Elizabeth went on seriously, "but I can fix him up."

I smiled. "Okay, Doctor Elizabeth."

Elizabeth left my room. She returned with her sewing box. She sat down on my bed and began stitching up Moosie. I sat next to her and rested my head against her shoulder. I watched the operation.

While Elizabeth worked, she said, "I guess you've been having a bad day today, haven't you, Karen?"

"The worst," I agreed.

"Everybody has bad days," Elizabeth told me. "You know what happened on my worst day ever?"

"What?" I asked. Somehow, I had not thought of Elizabeth having bad days.

"Well, I was about sixteen."

"Older than Kristy?"

"Yes," Elizabeth answered. "And older than Sam. But not as old as Charlie."

I nodded.

"And all in one day," Elizabeth said, "I flunked a test, my gym teacher yelled at me, I burned the chicken my family was having for dinner, I cut my hand, I had a fight with one of my sisters, and I lost my favorite earrings."

"That *is* pretty bad," I agreed.

"You know who else once had a bad day?" asked Elizabeth.

"Who?" I said.

"A little boy named Alexander. And there is a very funny book about his bad day. It's called *Alexander and the Terrible, Horrible, No Good, Very Bad Day.* Would you like to hear that story?"

"Yes," I answered. "And so would Moosie."

"Good," said Elizabeth, "because Moosie's operation is over and he's all well now. So why don't you wait here with him while I find the book? I think it's in David Michael's room."

"Okay," I replied. I held Moosie very gently until Elizabeth came back with the book.

We sat together on my bed and read it. It was funny and it was sad. Sometimes I laughed. Sometimes I said, "Alexander is just like me."

"How do you feel now?" Elizabeth asked me when the story was over.

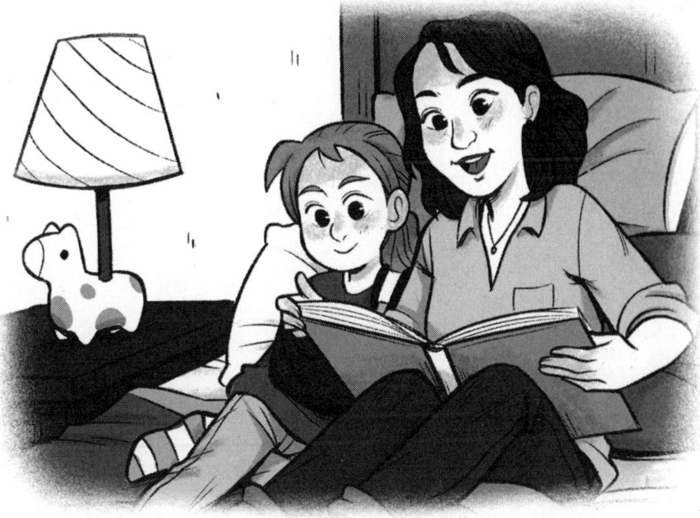

"Much better," I said. "I think Alexander's day was even worse than mine. The dentist found a cavity in Alexander's tooth. I've never had a cavity."

"You know what? I have an idea for how you could turn your bad day into a good day."

"How?" I asked.

"Why don't you pretend the day is just beginning? You could start all over again. Here, lie down on your bed."

I lay down. Then Elizabeth said, "Karen! Karen! Time to wake up!"

I yawned and stretched.

"Is it morning?" I asked.

Elizabeth and I laughed.

"Yes," said Elizabeth. "Time to start a new day."

"Okay. I just know today is going to be wonderful!" I exclaimed.

CHAPTER 12

I put Moosie on the bed. I covered him with Tickly. He needed to rest after his operation.

"Feel better," I whispered to Moosie as Elizabeth and I went downstairs.

"Guess what," said Elizabeth. "It's almost mail time. Why don't you run outside and see if Mr. Venta is coming?"

"Okay," I said.

Mr. Venta is our mailman. He is very nice. Sometimes he lets me ride down our street with him. I sit in his truck and open the mailboxes so Mr. Venta can slide the mail in. If a flag is up on a box, it means a letter is inside, waiting to be mailed. When we see one of those boxes, I let

Mr. Venta take the letter out first, and then put the mail in.

I like Mr. Venta almost as much as I like Mr. Tastee, the ice-cream man.

I stood on our front steps. I looked up and down the street. No mail truck. Maybe Hannie and Linny and David Michael would come home. I felt bad about yelling at Hannie. I wanted to tell her I was sorry. And I wanted to play with her.

But I did not see them, either.

I sat down on the steps. I watched a beetle in the grass. I read all the signatures on my cast. Then I counted them. Then—

I heard squeaky brakes. I looked up. There was the mail truck!

Mr. Venta was several houses away. Perfect. I could run to his truck, climb on, and ride back to my house!

I took off. I am not supposed to run fast with my cast on, so I ran slowly. I jogged to the mail truck. It was at the Werners' house.

"Hi, Mr. Ven—"

I stopped. Mr. Venta was not driving the truck. A woman was driving it. I had never seen her before.

"Do you live here?" asked the woman.

"No," I replied sadly. "I live down there." I pointed to our house.

Then I began walking home. I couldn't ask a stranger for a ride in the mail truck. That would not be safe. Besides, I only like riding with Mr. Venta.

I could feel my bad luck coming back again.

It's a new day, it's a new day, I reminded myself as I waited by our mailbox. *It isn't a bad day yet. Maybe something will come in the mail for me! Maybe I will get a letter . . . or a package! Even a sample would be good. I like samples of shampoo and hand lotion.*

The mail truck crept toward me. At last it pulled up at our box. I held my hands out, and the lady placed a stack of mail in them. On top of the stack was a package! I hoped it was for

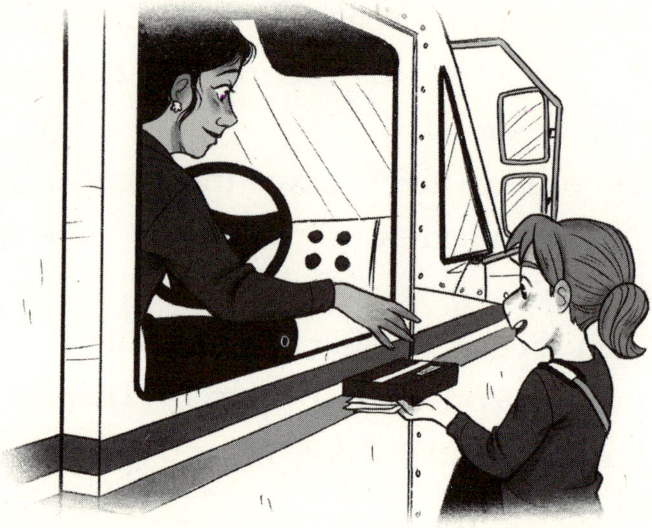

me, but I didn't look at the address. I would not look at it until I was sitting on our steps again. I would look at the rest of the mail first. Then I would look at the package. I would look at the return address, too. If I knew who it was from, maybe I could guess what it was.

"Thanks!" I called as the truck pulled away.

I carried the mail to our house. I was careful not to look at it. I sat down. I put the package under the letters. Then I looked at the letters. The first one was for Daddy. The second was for

Elizabeth. Then Elizabeth again, then Daddy, Daddy, Charlie, Elizabeth, Daddy, Elizabeth, David Michael, then two catalogues, and finally a magazine for Sam.

I was down to the package. I turned it over and read the address.

It was for Andrew.

CHAPTER 13

Hello! We're home!" called Daddy.

Daddy and Andrew came into the kitchen. They were home from the barber. I was sitting at the table watching Elizabeth make hamburger patties. Elizabeth had asked me what I wanted for dinner, and I had said, "Hamburgers, please."

The mail was on the kitchen counter.

"Hi, there," replied Elizabeth. "Andrew, you look very handsome."

I did not say anything. I did not think Andrew looked handsome. I thought he looked funny. The barber had cut his hair too short.

I did not want to hurt his feelings, even though he *had* gotten a package in the mail.

I was pretty mad about that package. In fact,

I was furious. How come Andrew got the prize in the Crunch-O cereal box *and* a package? If it was my bad day, it must have been Andrew's good day, maybe his best day.

The package was from Andrew's godparents. His godparents give him presents on his birthday and at Christmas and at lots of other times. Sometimes they send him a present for no reason at all.

I have godparents, too, and they do the same thing. But since today was my worst day and it was Andrew's best day, I did not get a present and he did.

Maybe Andrew's present would be very, very boring. Maybe it would be socks or a sweater or even underwear.

I tried to act happy for Andrew, though. "Guess what," I said to him. "You got a present from Uncle Lou and Aunt Ann."

"I did?!" cried Andrew. "Oh, boy!"

I gave Andrew the package. He ripped the paper off. Inside a white box he found two

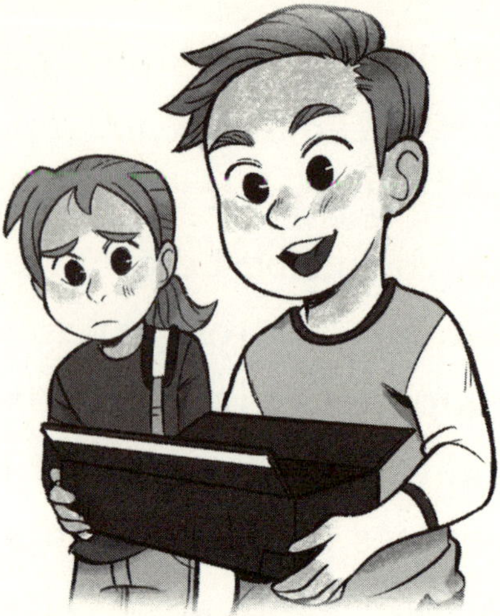

movies—*Lady and the Tramp* and *The Secret of NIMH.*

Those were not terrible, boring presents. They were wonderful presents!

I couldn't believe it.

"Wow!" cried Andrew. "New movies! Look Karen!"

"Yeah, I see."

"Let's go watch them right now!"

"No way," I replied.

"Why not?" asked Andrew.

"Because I don't want to watch movies with

an egghead. You look like an egghead, Andrew. I think I will call you Mr. Baldy from now on."

Andrew's eyes slowly filled with tears.

"Karen," said Daddy sharply, "apologize right now."

"No," I replied. "Mr. Baldy, you are spoiled. And you won't like the movies. That's the real reason I don't want to watch them. They are dumb and stupid and boring and bad."

"Are not!"

"Are too. You will hate those rats of NIMH. You will hate Nicodemus and Jenner. You will hate Mrs. Frisby, too. And Lady and Tramp and everybody in the other movie."

"I will not!"

"Will too!"

"Karen," said Daddy in a very loud voice, "go to your room. Right now. I know you're having a bad day, but you may not take it out on Andrew. Please stay in your room for twenty minutes."

"O-*kay*!" I shouted.

I stomped up to my room as loudly as I could.

CHAPTER 14

No fair, no fair, no fair.

It was not fair that I got sent to my room for having a bad day.

After I had stomped, stomped, stomped to my room, I grabbed my door and flung it—but I caught it just before it slammed. I shut it quietly. Daddy and Elizabeth do not like slamming doors.

I lay down on my bed with Moosie.

I cried for awhile.

I had done everything I could think of to make my bad day better. Elizabeth had even helped me to start it over. I thought I had been very patient.

The bad day was not my fault. I did not

mean to fall out of bed or leave my new jeans at Mommy's. And I could not help the Crunch-O prize package being empty or *Mr. Ed* not being on TV or Moosie being ripped. And I certainly couldn't help that Aunt Ann and Uncle Lou had sent Andrew a terrific present on his best day. Anyway, it might all be Morbidda Destiny's fault.

And now *I* was being punished.

I wiped my eyes and blew my nose. "How are you feeling, Moosie?" I asked. I looked at his scar. It was neat and tidy. I barely noticed it. "I guess you're feeling okay again, aren't you?"

I made Moosie nod his head.

After awhile, I got up and went to my mirror. I stood in front of it. I made the saddest face I could think of. I stuck out my lower lip and pretended I was about to cry.

"Everyone hates me," I said, and felt even sadder. "Kristy hates me because I acted like a baby. Daddy and Elizabeth and Andrew hate me because I was mean to Andrew. Hannie

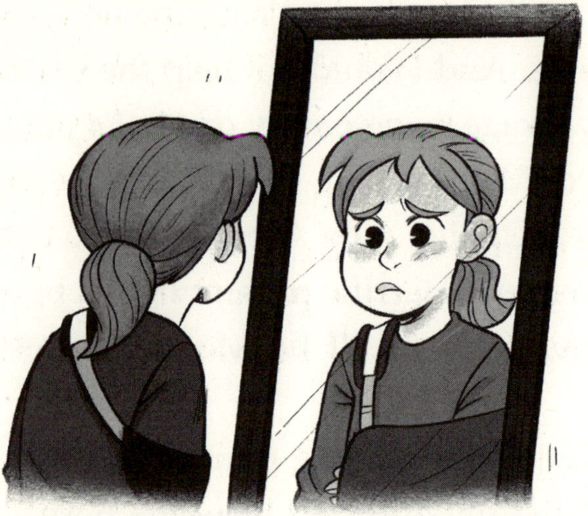

hates me because I yelled at her. Maybe Mr. Venta even hates me. Maybe that's why he wasn't driving the truck today."

Then I remembered a song. The worm song. "Nobody likes me," I sang sadly. "Everybody hates me. Guess I'll go eat worms. . . ."

Ew. Yuck. That was a really gross song.

I made an even sadder face and felt even sorrier for myself.

Then I flumped onto my bed. I picked up Moosie and pretended he was Andrew. "Karen, look at the new movies I got!" I made Moosie say in a high voice.

"You are so spoiled," I replied in my regular voice.

"Am not."

"Are too."

"Am not."

"Are too."

"Okay, I am spoiled. You're right."

"Let me have your movies," I said.

"No."

"Yes."

"No."

"All right. Here they are. They're yours."

"Thanks . . . Mr. Baldy."

That was how our fight should have gone. I sighed hugely.

I tiptoed to my door and opened it a crack. I listened. Nothing. I stuck my head into the hall. Nothing. I went out in the hall and peered between the railings of the bannister. Nothing. I couldn't see anyone or hear anything below.

So I went back in my room and just sat on my bed with Moosie in my lap. "Nobody likes me," I sang. "Everybody hates me. . . ."

I sang the song ten whole times at the top of my lungs before Daddy knocked on my door. He said my punishment was over. I had only been in my room for about fifteen minutes. I think he just wanted me to stop singing the worm song.

CHAPTER 15

As I was leaving my room, I thought I heard a noise. It sounded like bells. I ran back into my room and looked out the window.

Mr. Tastee was coming!

I grabbed some change that I keep in my jewelry box. Good luck at last! Mr. Tastee was coming just when my punishment was over, and I had enough money for an ice cream.

I ran downstairs.

"Here comes Mr. Tastee!" I shouted to whomever might be listening.

"Goody!" replied Andrew.

Both Andrew and Kristy followed me outside. We ran to the sidewalk and waved our hands.

Mr. Tastee was driving slowly up our street, bells clanging. Guess who was coming down the street in the other direction? Hannie, Linny, and David Michael. Their picnic was over. They threw their bicycles down on our lawn and waited with Andrew and Kristy and me. A few moments later, Amanda and Max Delaney joined us. They live across the street from us. Amanda is my friend.

While we waited for Mr. Tastee, I glanced at Hannie. Was she still mad? Hannie looked at me. She smiled a tiny smile. I smiled a tiny smile back. Maybe things would be okay. At least we were smiling.

Ding-ding-ding-ding!

Mr. Tastee had arrived!

He stopped his truck at the curb and got out.

"Hello, kids," he said. "Hi, Karen. Hi, Hannie."

"Hi, Mr. Tastee!" we answered.

We all crowded around the truck.

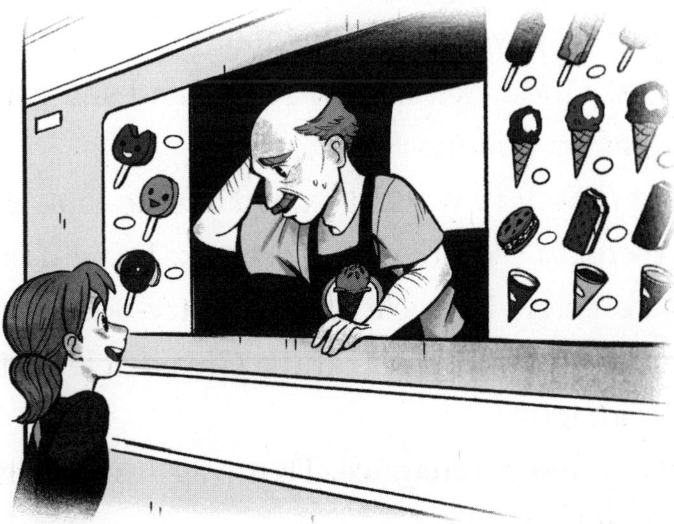

"Okay, okay! Form a line," said Mr. Tastee. "That will be much easier."

We made a line. Andrew was at the front. I was at the back. But I didn't care. I had ice-cream money. And in a few minutes, I would have a treat.

"Well, Andrew, what would you like?" asked Mr. Tastee. He adjusted his white hat.

"A double chocolate Popsicle, please."

"Right-o."

Mr. Tastee gave Andrew the Popsicle, and Andrew gave him some money.

Amanda Delaney was next, and she bought a toasted almond Popsicle.

What did I want? I leaned over to look at the ice-cream pictures on the truck. I saw a chocolate eclair Popsicle and a Nutty-Buddy cone and a rocket Popsicle and a Creamsicle and . . . Italian ices!

A cherry Italian ice. That was exactly what I wanted.

The line was growing shorter and shorter. Max and Linny and David Michael bought Nutty-Buddies. Hannie bought a Creamsicle.

At last—my turn.

"I'll have a cherry Italian ice, please," I said to Mr. Tastee.

"Right-o." Mr. Tastee rummaged around in the freezer in his truck. He looked and looked. At last he said, "I'm sorry, Karen. I'm out of cherry."

"No cherry?!" I cried.

"No. But there's lemon and grape and—"

"I wanted cherry!"

"I'm very sorry, Karen."

I couldn't help it. I burst into tears and ran inside.

CHAPTER 16

Karen! Dinnertime!"

Kristy was calling me. I was in my room rocking Moosie. I was not a bit hungry.

"I'm not hungry!" I yelled back.

A few moments later, Elizabeth called to me. "Karen, we'd like you to come to dinner, please."

"But I'm not hungry," I replied. I had not even had an Italian ice and I still wasn't hungry.

"Please come anyway."

I slogged downstairs. I dragged myself into the dining room. I slumped into my chair. I was the last person to sit down at the table.

Everybody was there: Daddy, Elizabeth,

Charlie, Sam, Kristy, David Michael, and Andrew. They had already been served. A plate of food was at my place.

I stared at it. There was a hamburger and a baked potato and salad. I like all of those things. But I put my chin in my hands. I didn't want to eat. My bad day had tired me out. I was too tired to eat.

"Well," said Daddy, after he had eaten a bite of his hamburger, "I guess you had a bad day today, didn't you, Karen?"

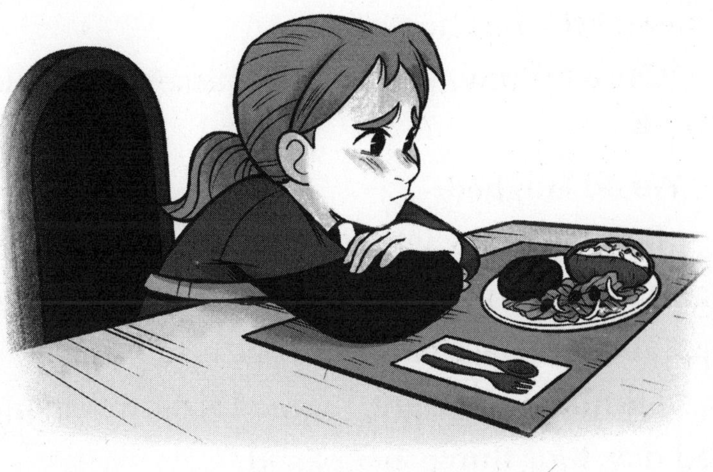

I nodded.

"No Crunch-O prize and no cherry Italian ice," said Andrew sadly.

"No present and no *Mr. Ed* and I fell out of bed and Moosie got ripped," I added.

"Last week," spoke up Sam, "I had a bad day. I lost my homework and I stepped on Boo-Boo's tail. I felt awful."

"That's just two bad things, though," Kristy pointed out. "Once, my chair tipped over in English class and I'd forgotten my lunch money and my locker got stuck so I couldn't open it and I missed the bus home."

"Once I threw up in a school assembly," said Charlie.

We all laughed.

"But you know what?" I said suddenly. "I've had the worst bad day of all. More bad things happened to me than to anyone else."

"I think you're right," agreed Kristy. "On my bad day, four things happened."

"Seven bad things happened to me on my worst day," said Daddy.

"How about you, Elizabeth?" I asked. "How many bad things happened on the day you told me about while you were operating on Moosie?"

"Let's see," said Elizabeth. She paused. "Six bad things."

"Okay," I replied. "Now let me count up my bad things." I used my fingers to help me. "I had a scary dream. I fell out of bed. I couldn't find my jeans. No Crunch-O prize. No *Mr. Ed*. Shannon wouldn't play with me. Then Boo-Boo wouldn't play, either. I had a fight with Hannie. I sort of had a fight with you, Kristy. Moosie got ripped. There was no Mr. Venta. I didn't get any mail. I got sent to my room for being mean to Andrew. And there was no cherry Italian ice. Fourteen bad things. . . . *Fourteen!*" (I left out the part about Morbidda Destiny's spell, because grown-ups don't like to hear about witch things.)

"Gosh," said Kristy, "if there were a prize for bad days, you would win it, Karen."

"I think," I said, "that this is the first good thing that's happened to me today. I set a bad-day record!"

CHAPTER 17

As soon as I realized that I had set a bad-day record, I began to feel better. I even felt hungry. So I ate every bite of my dinner.

"Mmm," said Charlie as my family and I were cleaning up the kitchen later, "you know what would taste good right now?"

"What?" I asked.

"Ice cream."

"I don't think we have any."

"I know. That's why Sam and I were wondering if you would come to Sullivan's Sweets with us tonight. We would like you to be our date."

"You want to go to the ice-cream parlor?!" I cried. "Just the three of us?"

Charlie nodded. "You and Sam and I didn't

get any ice cream from Mr. Tastee this afternoon. So we should take care of that. Will you come?"

"Sure! If it's okay with Daddy and Elizabeth."

"It's okay," they said at the same time.

"Then let's go," said Sam.

Boy, did I feel grown-up. Charlie is old enough to drive, so we could go to Sullivan's Sweets all by ourselves. Sam sat in the front seat of the car with Charlie. I sat in the back. When we left our house, it was still light out. I hoped somebody would see me. It wasn't everyday I got to ride in the car to the ice-cream parlor with my big brothers.

Charlie drove us downtown. He parked right in front of Sullivan's Sweets. We went inside and sat down at a small round table.

"So far, so good," I whispered to Sam and Charlie. "Nothing bad has happened."

Sam grinned. "Keep it up, kid."

Soon a waiter came to our table. "What'll it be?" he asked us.

Please, please, please don't be out of chocolate sodas, I thought.

"Karen?" asked Charlie. "Have you made up your mind?"

"I'll bet you don't have any chocolate sodas left, do you," I said.

"Of course we do. We can make anything," replied the waiter. "One chocolate soda, coming right up."

"Goody!" I exclaimed.

Sam and Charlie each ordered a hot-fudge

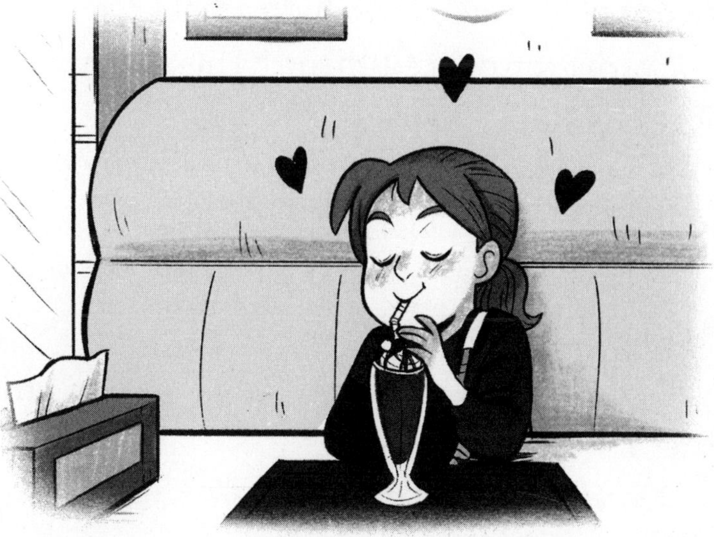

sundae, and then the waiter left. When he came back, one chocolate soda and two hot-fudge sundaes were on his tray.

"So far, so good," I said again.

Slurp, slurp, slurp. I sipped my soda. It was the best one I'd ever had.

We were just finishing our treats when the door to Sullivan's opened. In came two big boys and two big girls.

"Hey!" exclaimed Charlie. "Hi, you guys!"

The kids came over to our table. They were friends of Charlie's from high school.

Charlie introduced them. "This is John and Greg and Kate and Sandy," he said.

"And who's this?" asked John, pointing to me. "Is this your older sister, Charlie?"

I beamed. John thought I was older than Charlie!

"Nah," replied Charlie, "this is my little sister Karen."

"Do you have a license, Karen?" asked John. "Wait, don't tell me. You drove here, right?"

I started to giggle. "No!" I cried. "People don't get licenses when they're six."

"You're only *six?* I thought you were *twenty*-six."

"No!" I said, still laughing.

Charlie and his friends talked about school for awhile. Then his friends sat down at another table. It was time for us to leave.

"Good-bye!" I called as we left Sullivan's.

"Good-bye!" called John and Greg and Kate and Sandy.

"Boy, thanks, Charlie. Thanks, Sam," I said. "Not a single thing went wrong at the ice-cream parlor. So that's the second good thing that's happened today."

We climbed into the car and drove home.

CHAPTER 18

Charlie pulled into our driveway. I jumped out of the car and ran inside. "Daddy! Elizabeth! Kristy!" I exclaimed. "Guess what!"

The rest of my family was watching TV in the den. But when they saw me, they turned off the television.

"What is it, sweetie?" asked Elizabeth.

"Everything went right! Charlie found a parking place in front of Sullivan's. And they had chocolate sodas. I wanted a chocolate soda more than anything. Even more than a cherry Italian ice. And then Charlie's friends came in, and one of them asked if I was Charlie's older sister! Then he thought I was twenty-six!"

Elizabeth and Daddy laughed.

"That's wonderful, honey," said Daddy. "And now, guess what time it is."

"Time to get ready for bed?" I asked.

"Exactly. Time for Andrew and David Michael, too."

My brothers' eyes met mine. We grinned at each other. "Let's go!" I said.

We ran up the stairs. We have a bedtime secret. No one knows about it but us. It's the special way we brush our teeth.

The three of us gathered in the bathroom. We loaded our brushes with toothpaste. Then

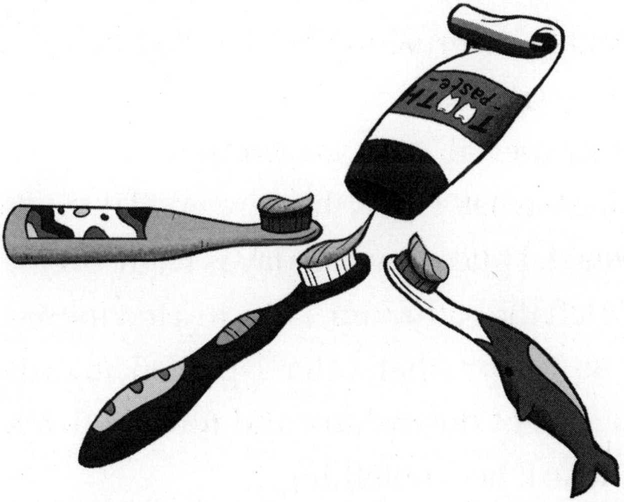

we brushed and brushed and brushed until our mouths were just full of foam. I had to brush left-handed because of my cast.

When we could not keep the foam in our mouths any longer, I said, "Okay, one, two, three, spit," only it sounded like, "Unh, two, fee, pit."

We spat.

I had never seen so much toothpaste foam in the sink. Neither had David Michael nor Andrew.

"We did it!" I said. "We set another foam record."

"I'll say," agreed David Michael.

"And I was brushing left-handed. So this is a very special record."

"*Very* special," echoed Andrew.

"Guess what. This is the third good thing that's happened. I guess my bad day is really over."

We left the bathroom. I was in a terrific mood. I felt so happy, that, after I put on my nightgown, I went downstairs and found Elizabeth. I had to ask her something.

"Elizabeth," I said, "before I go to bed, may I do three things? They're really important. And they won't take a long time."

"All right," agreed Elizabeth.

CHAPTER 19

My three important things were apologies. I needed to say "I'm sorry" to Andrew and to Hannie and to Kristy. I started with Andrew, since he had to go to bed soon.

"Andrew?" I said. I stood at the door to his room. He was sitting on the floor, looking at a picture book.

"Yeah?" said Andrew.

"Can I come in?"

Andrew nodded.

Then he and I sat on his bed. I drew in a deep breath. "Andrew," I said, "I'm really really really sorry I called you an egghead and Mr. Baldy. That was not nice at all. It's not your fault I had a rotten day."

"That's okay," said Andrew.

"You know what? Today Elizabeth read me a story. It was about a boy who has an awful day. It's called *Alexander and the Terrible, Horrible, No Good, Very Bad Day.* It's David Michael's book. Do you want me to read it to you? If I read it, you might understand how I felt."

"Okay," said Andrew.

I borrowed the book from David Michael. Then I read it to my little brother. "You see?" I said. "The worse the day is, the crosser you feel."

Andrew nodded. "I see. . . . Karen?"

"Yeah?"

"You can still have half my tattoos. And you can watch my new movies whenever you want."

"Thanks, Andrew."

I left Andrew's room. It was time for my next apology. I went into the kitchen. I called up Hannie.

"Hi, Hannie," I said. "It's me, Karen."

Hannie didn't say anything.

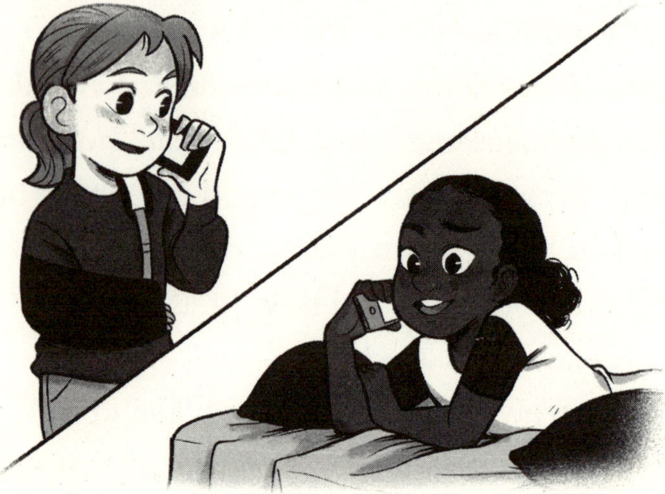

"I know you're mad," I went on. "I'm sorry I called you a toad. But you know what? Today was my worst day ever. It was so bad, I set a bad-day record. Fourteen bad things happened."

"Fourteen?" cried Hannie.

"Yup." I listed them for her. Then I told her about the good things. Well, not about the foam record, since that is a secret. But I told her the other things.

"A big guy asked if you were Charlie's older sister?" squeaked Hannie. "That is so, so cool."

"I know," I said. "Then he thought I was twenty-six!"

"Karen!" called Elizabeth. "Time for bed."

"I have to go, Hannie," I told her, "but I'll see you tomorrow, okay? We can play dolls. And I won't call you a toad."

"Deal," said Hannie, and we hung up.

Elizabeth was standing in the doorway to the kitchen. "Do you want Kristy to put you to bed?" she asked.

Kristy usually puts me to bed.

"Yes," I answered. "I'll say good-night to you and Daddy now."

"Okay." Elizabeth took my hand. We walked into the den.

I crawled into Daddy's lap and kissed his nose. "Good-night," I said.

"Good-night," said Daddy.

Then I gave him a butterfly kiss with my eyelashes.

"Elizabeth?" I said as I got out of Daddy's lap. "Can I tell you something?"

"Of course." Elizabeth sat down.

I put my hands around one of her ears and whispered, "Thank you."

Elizabeth put *her* hands around one of *my* ears. "For what?" she whispered back.

I giggled. "For fixing Moosie and reading the story about Alexander to me."

"You're welcome," Elizabeth replied.

Then we gave each other butterfly kisses and I went upstairs.

CHAPTER 20

Karen! Karen!" Kristy was calling me from upstairs.

"Coming!" I answered.

I ran up the stairs. Kristy had just put Andrew to bed. He goes to bed first since he's the youngest. After I go to bed, it's David Michael's turn.

Kristy was waiting in my room. I climbed into bed and hugged Moosie.

"Well," said Kristy, "what story shall we read? *The Witch Next Door*?"

The Witch Next Door is my all-time favorite story. I did want to hear it. But not right away. I had something to say. It was time for my third apology.

"Before we read a book," I told my big sister, "I have something to say to you."

"You do? What?"

"I'm sorry. I'm sorry about the checkers game. I wasn't nice to you."

"I *was* letting you win, though," said Kristy, "and that wasn't nice of me, either."

"But you were *trying* to be nice," I pointed out. "I was just feeling too awful to notice. So I'm sorry."

"In that case," said Kristy, "I accept your apology. I promise I'll never let you win again, though. The next time you win, it will be because you played a good game."

"Maybe the next time I win will be on a good day!" I exclaimed. "If today was my worst day, then some time I will have a best day. That will probably be a checkers-winning day."

"I hope so," said Kristy. "Now how about a story?"

"Okay, but you choose. Any book you want."

(I know Kristy gets tired of reading *The Witch Next Door.*)

"Really?" said Kristy. "How about if we begin a chapter book? I could start reading *Charlotte's Web* to you. You would really like it."

"Okay," I agreed, "but do I have that book?"

"No, I do. I'll go get it. I'll be right back."

While Kristy was in her room, I talked to Moosie. "You're going to hear a new story," I told him. "Try to listen quietly. No interrupting."

Kristy came back with the book. "Did anything bad happen while I was gone?" she teased me.

"Oh, Kristy," I said.

Kristy read the first chapter of *Charlotte's Web.* Then she told me about the rest of the book. The story was going to be about a girl named Fern Arable, who lives on a farm, and her pet pig Wilbur and a clever spider named Charlotte A. Cavatica. Kristy was right. I would like the book.

When Kristy finished the first chapter, she closed *Charlotte's Web*.

"Do you think pigs ever have bad days?" I asked her.

"Wilbur does. You'll see"

"What about witches?" I asked. "Do you think they ever have bad days?"

"Oh, sure," replied my sister. "They mix up their potions all wrong and their spells go ker-flooey and their broomsticks won't fly."

Kristy and I laughed.

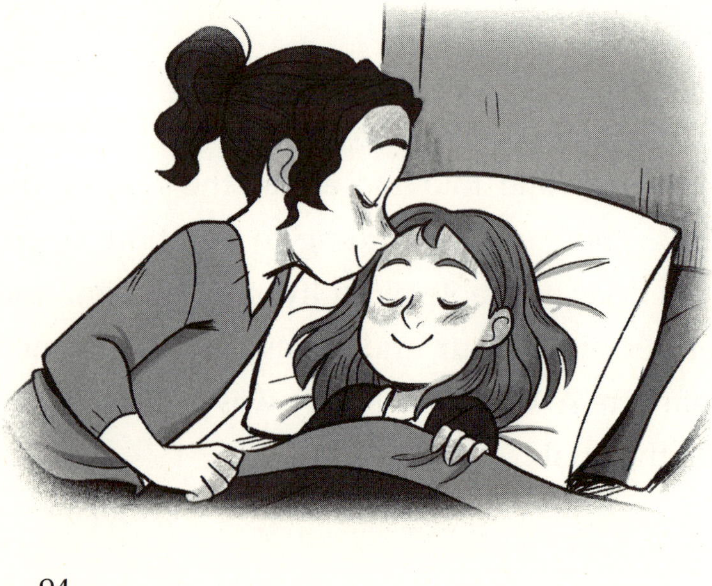

Then I snuggled under the covers. Kristy kissed me good-night. Then she kissed Moosie. She turned on my nightlight. As she was leaving the room she said, "I'm *sure* tomorrow will be a good day."

What a relief. I could not think of anything nicer.

"If that is true," I explained to Kristy, "then that is the fourth good thing about my bad day."

"Good-night, Karen."

"Good-night, Kristy."

About the Author

Ann M. Martin's The Baby-sitters Club has sold over 190 million copies and inspired a generation of young readers. Her novels include the Newbery Honor Book *A Corner of the Universe, A Dog's Life,* and the Main Street series. She lives in upstate New York.

Keep reading for a sneak peek at the next Baby-sitters Little Sister book!

Karen's Kittycat Club

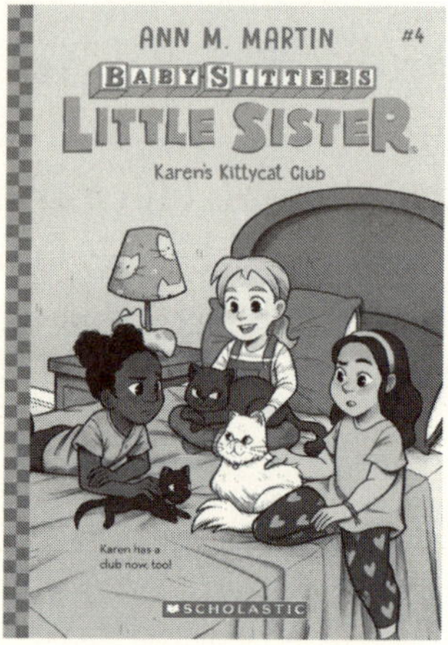

"What is it?" I shouted.

I stood up. I saw Hannie running across our lawn.

"Guess what? Guess what?" she called.

I began jumping up and down. That was how excited Hannie was making me. "I can't guess. Tell me," I cried. "Tell me quick!"

Hannie slowed to a stop. She could hardly

catch her breath. "We," she began, and then she had to start over. "We — we got a kitten!"

"A kitten?! Oh, Hannie. You are so lucky!"

"Linny and I have always wanted a cat," said Hannie. Linny is Hannie's older brother. He's eight. He and David Michael are friends. Hannie is seven. We're in the same class at school. (I skipped first grade.) Sari, Hannie's little sister, is just two.

"What did you name him?" I asked.

"Her," Hannie corrected me. "She's a her. And her name is Pat."

"Oh!" I exclaimed. "So when she's all grown up she'll be Pat the cat."

"Right," replied Hannie. "Pat the cat, Noodle the poodle, and Myrtle the turtle."

"Three pets," I said.

Hannie nodded proudly.

I could not help thinking again about how lucky Andrew and I are to be two-twos and have more pets than any of my friends. Maybe that wasn't a nice thing to think, but I thought it anyway.

"Karen, come over and meet Pat," said Hannie.

"Okay," I replied. I stuck my head in our front door. I told Daddy and Elizabeth where I was going. Then Hannie and I ran to her house.

"Pat is on the sun porch," Hannie told me. "We put all her stuff there. We put her toys and food and litter box on the floor. We spread out an old sweater for her to sleep on. I think she feels safe on the porch. She's too little to go roaming around the house." (Hannie's house is as big as Daddy's.)

Hannie and I tiptoed through the door to the porch.

"She might be asleep," Hannie whispered.

We checked the sweater. No Pat.

"Sometimes she hides," said Hannie.

We peered under the chairs and tables. No Pat.

Then something furry brushed against my ankle. I looked down. There was a fuzzy black kitten. She was carrying a toy in her mouth.

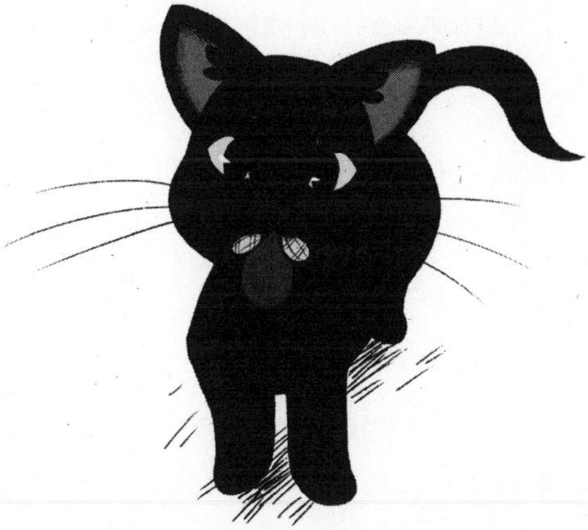

"Aw, Hannie," I exclaimed. "Look at her! She's so cute."

Hannie grinned. She and I tossed Pat's toy around for her. While we were playing, I thought of something.

"Hey, Hannie," I said. "It's neat that you have a cat."

"I know. Pat is our very first one."

"But there's something even better. Now you and Amanda and I all have cats," I pointed out to her. "We have Pat, Priscilla, and Boo-Boo. And Rocky at the little house."

"Yeah," said Hannie. She didn't sound too

interested. I guessed that was because she doesn't like Amanda very much.

But *I* was interested. Hannie and Amanda and I live right near each other. And now we all have cats.

"Look!" said Hannie. "Look what Pat can do."

Hannie held up a piece of string. She dangled it above Pat. Pat leaped up on her hind legs. She batted at the string.

I began to giggle. "Pat's dancing!" I cried.

Hannie laughed, too.

We let Pat dance until she got tired. Then she lay down on the sweater and fell asleep. Just like that.

"She's so cute," I said to Hannie. I think I had already said that about three thousand times.

"Yeah," agreed Hannie softly.

"I better go," I told her. "It's lunchtime. I'll see you later."

"Okay," replied Hannie. "See you!"

I left Hannie's house.

I was getting an idea.

Don't miss any of the books in the Baby-sitters Little Sister series by Ann M. Martin—available as ebooks

#1	Karen's Witch
#2	Karen's Roller Skates
#3	Karen's Worst Day
#4	Karen's Kittycat Club
#5	Karen's School Picture
#6	Karen's Little Sister
#7	Karen's Birthday
#8	Karen's Haircut
#9	Karen's Sleepover
#10	Karen's Grandmothers
#11	Karen's Prize
#12	Karen's Ghost
#13	Karen's Surprise
#14	Karen's New Year
#15	Karen's in Love
#16	Karen's Goldfish
#17	Karen's Brothers
#18	Karen's Home Run
#19	Karen's Good-bye
#20	Karen's Carnival
#21	Karen's New Teacher
#22	Karen's Little Witch
#23	Karen's Doll
#24	Karen's School Trip
#25	Karen's Pen Pal
#26	Karen's Ducklings
#27	Karen's Big Joke
#28	Karen's Tea Party
#29	Karen's Cartwheel
#30	Karen's Kittens
#31	Karen's Bully
#32	Karen's Pumpkin Patch
#33	Karen's Secret
#34	Karen's Snow Day
#35	Karen's Doll Hospital
#36	Karen's New Friend
#37	Karen's Tuba
#38	Karen's Big Lie
#39	Karen's Wedding
#40	Karen's Newspaper
#41	Karen's School:
#42	Karen's Pizza Party
#43	Karen's Toothache
#44	Karen's Big Weekend
#45	Karen's Twin
#46	Karen's Baby-sitter
#47	Karen's Kite
#48	Karen's Two Families
#49	Karen's Stepmother
#50	Karen's Lucky Penny
#51	Karen's Big Top
#52	Karen's Mermaid
#53	Karen's School Bus
#54	Karen's Candy
#55	Karen's Magician
#56	Karen's Ice Skates
#57	Karen's School Mystery
#58	Karen's Ski Trip
#59	Karen's Leprechaun
#60	Karen's Pony
#61	Karen's Tattletale
#62	Karen's New Bike
#63	Karen's Movie
#64	Karen's Lemonade Stand
#65	Karen's Toys
#66	Karen's Monsters
#67	Karen's Turkey Day
#68	Karen's Angel

#69 Karen's Big Sister
#70 Karen's Grandad
#71 Karen's Island Adventure
#72 Karen's New Puppy
#73 Karen's Dinosaur
#74 Karen's Softball Mystery
#75 Karen's County Fair
#76 Karen's Magic Garden
#77 Karen's School Surprise
#78 Karen's Half Birthday
#79 Karen's Big Fight
#80 Karen's Christmas Tree
#81 Karen's Accident
#82 Karen's Secret Valentine
#83 Karen's Bunny
#84 Karen's Big Job
#85 Karen's Treasure
#86 Karen's Telephone Trouble
#87 Karen's Pony Camp
#88 Karen's Puppet Show
#89 Karen's Unicorn
#90 Karen's Haunted House
#91 Karen's Pilgrim
#92 Karen's Sleigh Ride
#93 Karen's Cooking Contest
#94 Karen's Snow Princess
#95 Karen's Promise
#96 Karen's Big Move
#97 Karen's Paper Route
#98 Karen's Fishing Trip
#99 Karen's Big City Mystery
#100 Karen's Book
#101 Karen's Chain Letter
#102 Karen's Black Cat
#103 Karen's Movie Star
#104 Karen's Christmas Carol
#105 Karen's Nanny
#106 Karen's President
#107 Karen's Copycat
#108 Karen's Field Day
#109 Karen's Show and Share
#110 Karen's Swim Meet
#111 Karen's Spy Mystery
#112 Karen's New Holiday
#113 Karen's Hurricane
#114 Karen's Chicken Pox
#115 Karen's Runaway Turkey
#116 Karen's Reindeer
#117 Karen's Mistake
#118 Karen's Figure Eight
#119 Karen's Yo-Yo
#120 Karen's Easter Parade
#121 Karen's Gift
#122 Karen's Cowboy

Super Specials

#1 Karen's Wish
#2 Karen's Plane Trip
#3 Karen's Mystery
#4 Karen, Hannie, and Nancy: The Three Musketeers
#5 Karen's Baby
#6 Karen's Campout

DON'T MISS THE BABY-SITTERS CLUB GRAPHIC NOVELS!

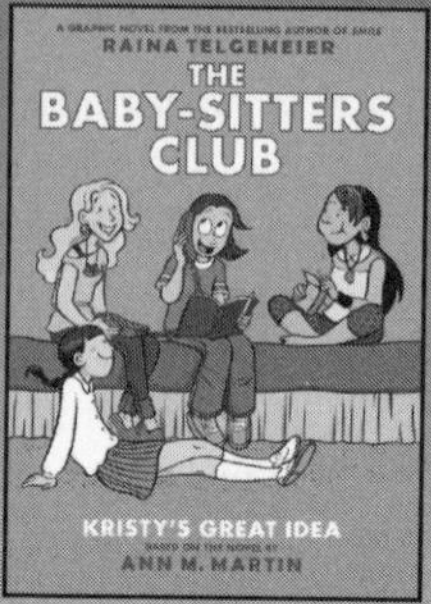

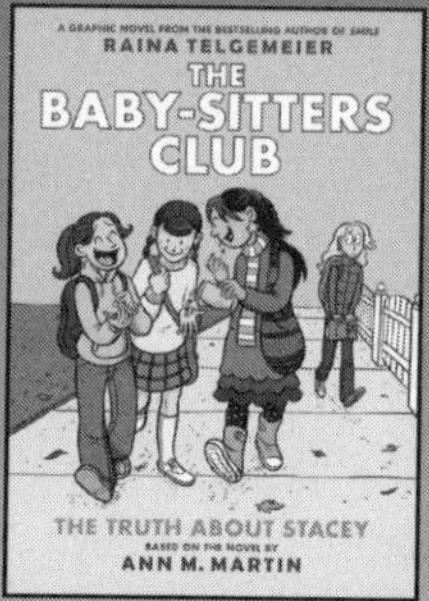

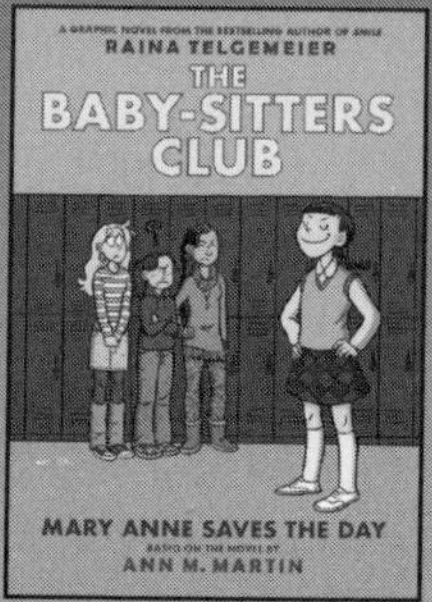

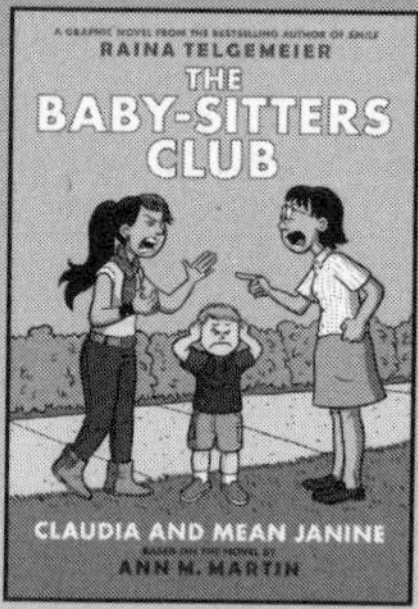

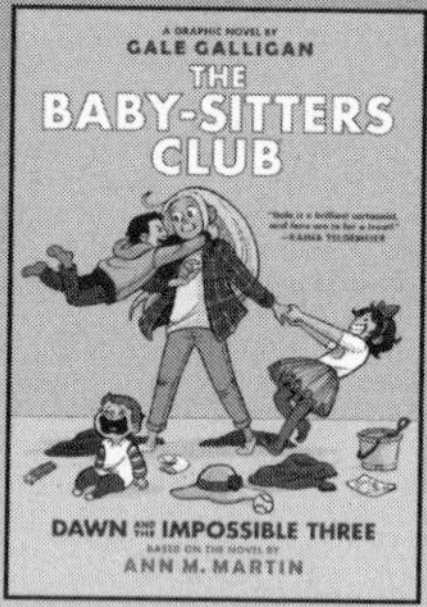

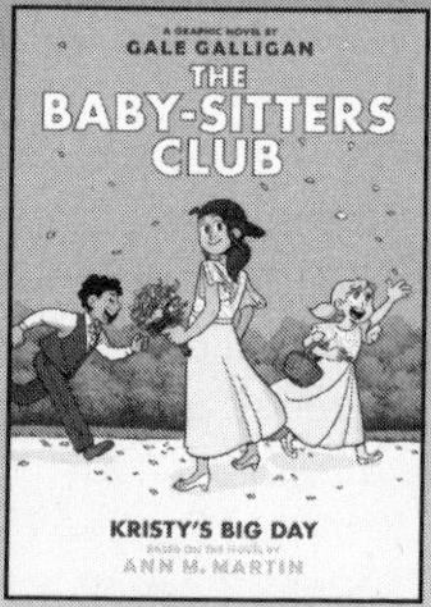

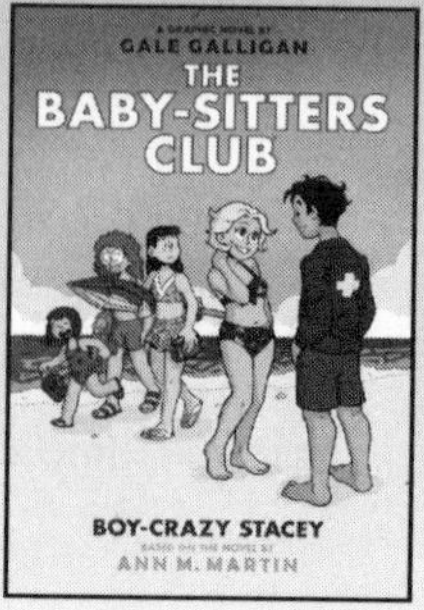

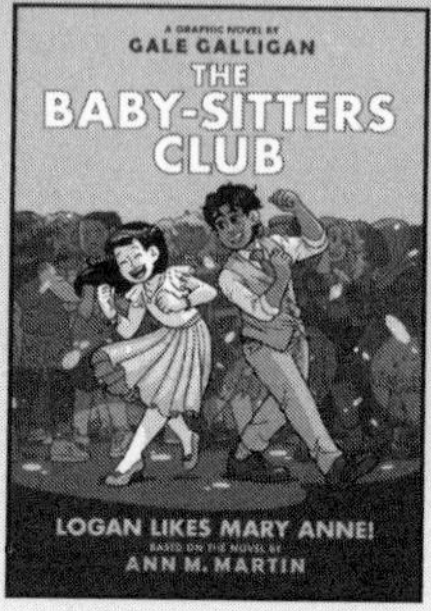

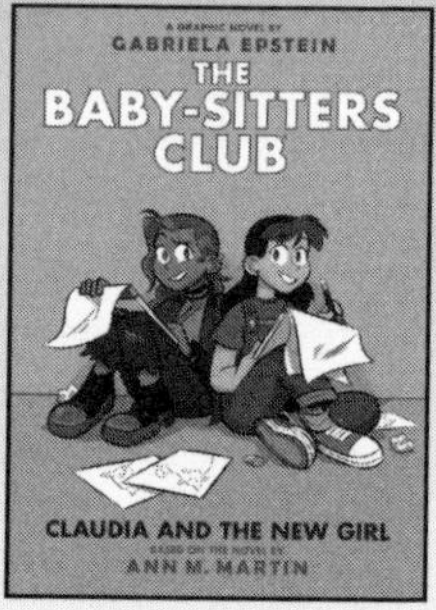

graphix

AN IMPRINT OF

SCHOLASTIC

scholastic.com/graphix

BS

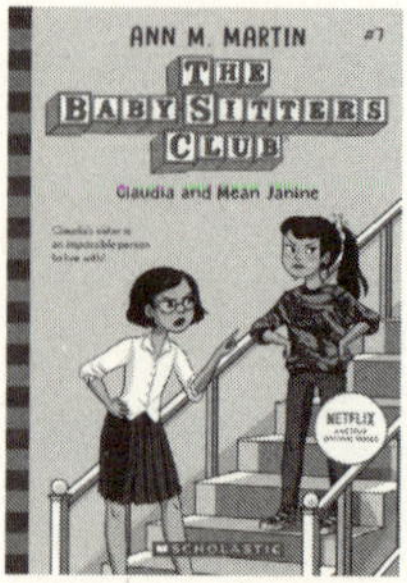

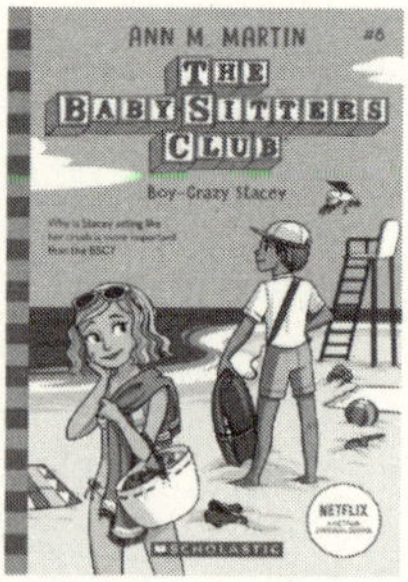

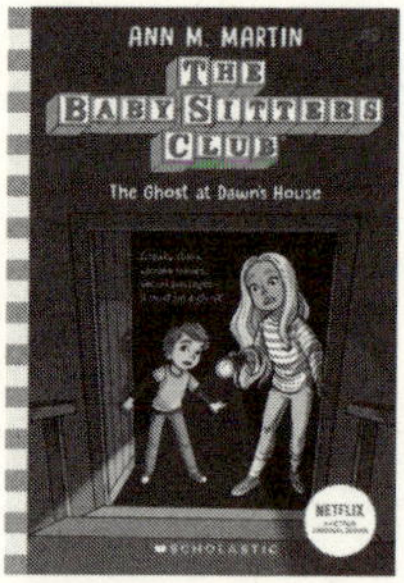

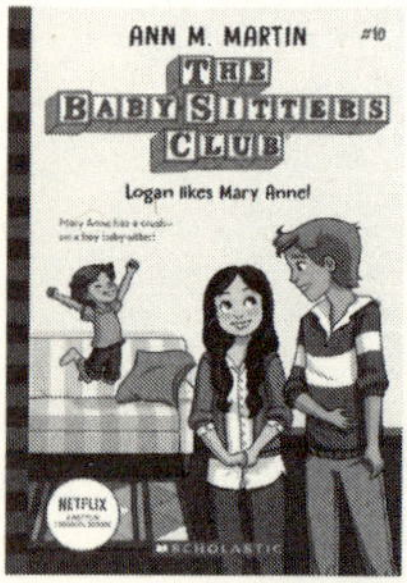

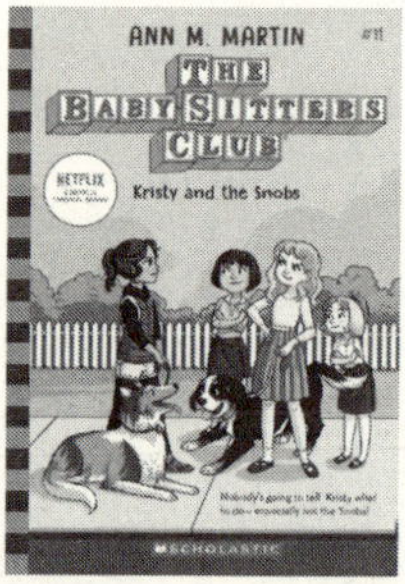

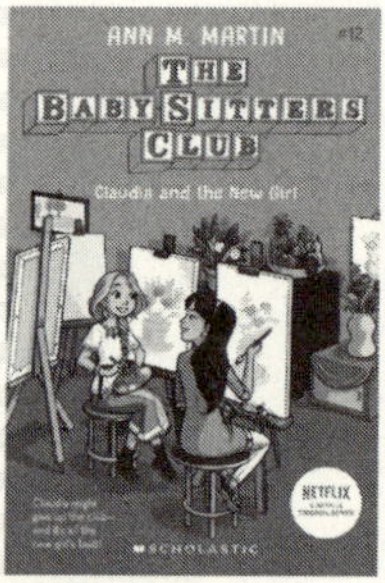

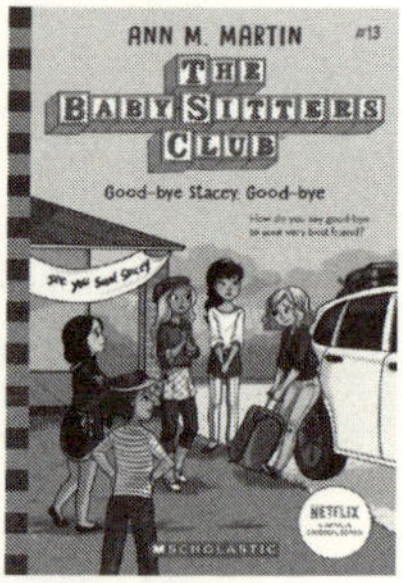

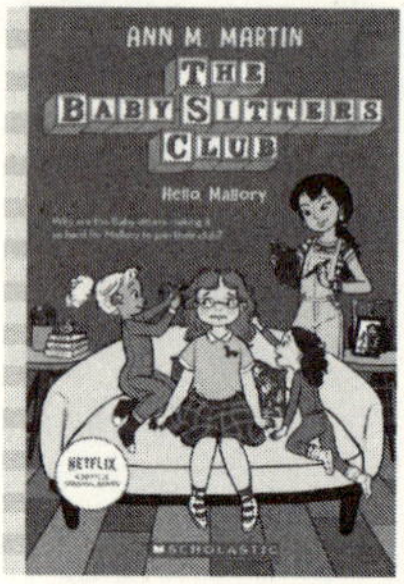

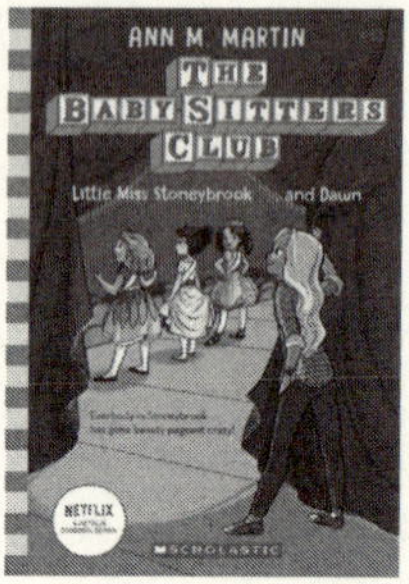

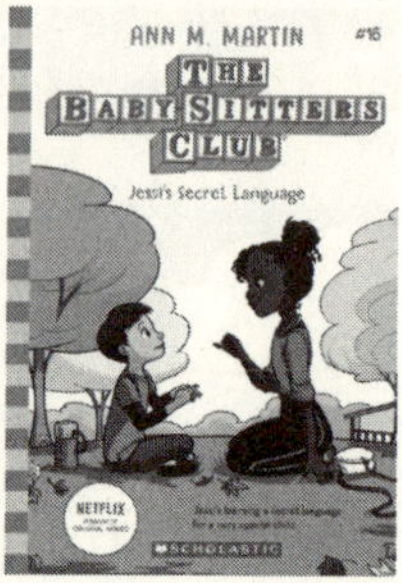

And many more!